AF255513

All the Birds Were Invited

to a Feast in the Sky

All the Birds Were Invited

to a Feast in the Sky

SOUKEYNA OSEI-BONSU

First published 2021 by Lote Tree Press

www.lotetreepress.com

ISBN 978-1-9162488-6-1

© Soukeyna Osei-Bonsu

All right reserved

A CIP catalogue record for this book is available from the British Library

بِسْمِ اللَّهِ الرَّحْمَٰنِ الرَّحِيمِ

for the family

'"Once upon a time," she began, "all the birds were invited to a feast in the sky"'
- Things Fall Apart, Chinua Achebe

'In the mornings I drank the dew that fell from the magnolia;
In the evenings ate the petals that dropped from the chrysanthemums.
If only my mind can be truly beautiful,
It matters nothing that I often faint for famine.'
-Li sao, Qu Yuan

acknowledgements

i would like to thank my family, my predecessors and all the individuals and circumstances both positive and negative that taught me to write

Contents

for the family 9

acknowledgements 11

part one: shedding weight, breathing light 15

the ghuraf 16

khimar 18

going home 17.02-23-02 20

all the birds were invited to a feast in the sky 22

dahlia* 24

synchronicity 26

concerning the sweetness of our mothers 28

my grandmother cooked a blossom 30

rosary 32

origami lungs 34

clay 36

silkworm 38

happiness   40

part two: by africa, the iridescence of her beauty   43

by the quiver of an arrow   44

ruins   46

equator   48

accra sunset   50

the carpet weaver   52

boats and bilqees   54

the textbooks of the scholars   56

the alien   58

wagadou   60

mahogany   62

ohema, daughter of the sun   64

part one: shedding weight, breathing light

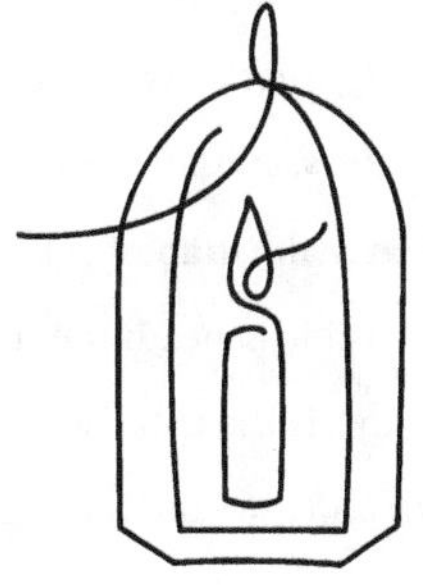

the ghuraf

gilded butterflies, gilded roses, gilded veins

serve a function here, where the perfume of past praise

colours the stars, and where green birds flitter between nests

dangling from the Throne of light, illuminating ancient whispers

into earth, to tangible seeds. this is the tribe. we are the few of the latter

with most of the former. we are the tribe. this is the people

of delectable delight, the hush of bliss is too sweet to withstand.

the melody of gold, the aura of soaring ruby

the scent of saffron soil, the forgotten tears of the downtrodden

alchemised to crystal, the same crystallisation of glinting palaces

upon built palaces, the stacked manhattan of celestial beauty

a silver bombay, the marrow visible beneath the surface of giants

the same giants who declare: this is the tribe. we are the people

of *salām*. we are the people of *iḥsān*. we are the elegant tribe

of elongated necks, transcending time and space, the clinks

of our glasses and the echo of our laughter, faintly detectable

in the blackness of the cosmos

khimar

cascading fabric, a lifeline coiled floating from a cloud

knotted to the rope of God, this barrier, this strange refuge

a hushed memory of who i was before sudden birth

ethereal recognition was the day i looked in the mirror

draped in a starless sky, something foreign, familiar,

something shifting, stopping my heart, and startling my breath, a silent

dimension i couldn't perceive, perhaps one day

i'll articulate it. whispers of the deceased sewn into sacred cloth

i remember them as i walk, the swish

their tired hymn. tug at you, wrapped with you, white knuckled grip,

because you are life, in a dream state i tread through

tottenham court road. home at last, return

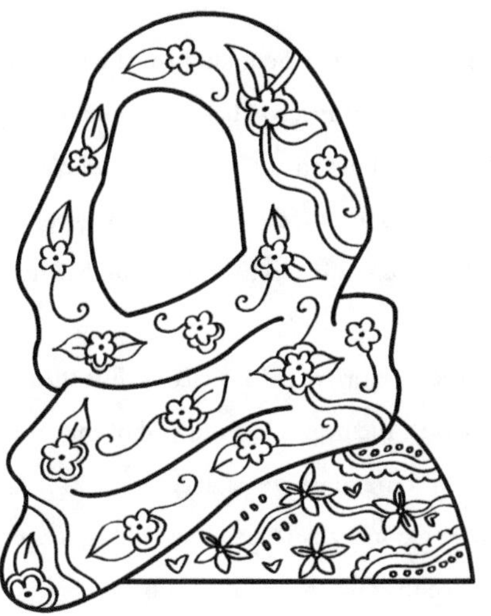

going home 17.02-23-02

last night the moon set in my lap, i couldn't smile because i felt as though

the soil had already parted for me, so i held it in a kind of contemplation

strange wonders often befall us on autumn nights, when auburn plants

regress their swell, and nostalgia wakes you for a long-passed term time

but i couldn't think of these things when the moon balanced across my thighs;

only of You-

so when the sea spittle rose up, to form a city against the night

i knew then that marked the beginning and end of my time here-

now i'm going home. home to where parakeets

flash neon-green over gloomy skies - here the tail feathers that flitter

across high road, leave the faint musk of a baobab

all the birds were invited to a feast in the sky

a bank in the sky
or a ministry of words
will determine our lives

yawa's father's cousin's
gleaming eyes told her and her mother
"i am a messenger"
"those who try to harm you are
inspired by the devil"
"and the rest is from God"

that day
all the birds
were invited to a feast in the sky,
morning mist danced with the breath
of mami's "*ameen*"
at the swelling of new seed

akosua watered it:
"yawa you were born alone, how can you rely
on a human when you are alone?"

three orbits, three turmoils pass
thirty kilograms of chaos
now bloats her form

no mind;

a vine has tied the thrumming heart

and is now pushing out

of yawa's mouth

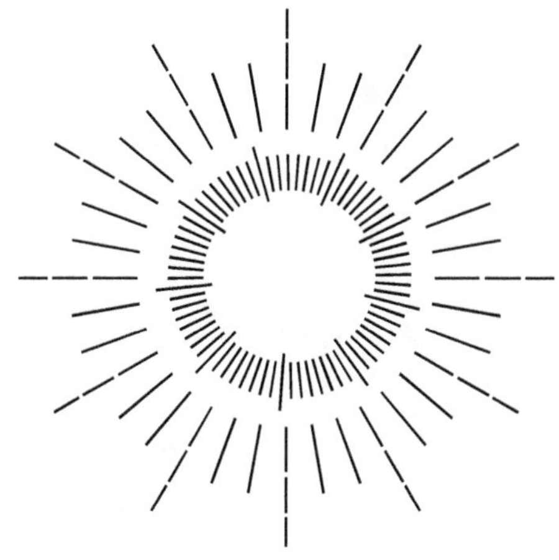

dahlia*

today i am a dahlia
i have extended my two feet
and i have chosen to surf
on the face of the sun

"we must dare to invent the future"
so i picture petals unravelling
in this short time here
and giving nurturing life
to black nobles who have not seen the grapevines

coiling across their thrones yet
and i picture the home that will never end
inside the pink hue of a hollowed pearl
the swirl of incense burning to raise my spirit
into annihilation

tonight i am a dahlia,
i have invented a dream that seems it could come true
so i work and pray that the fruits of this moon
that has risen across my iris

continues to glow a path
that will take me
to everlasting
bliss

*first published in The Drinking Gourd

synchronicity

a verdant word has dripped

into a glass of water

and billowed to the bottom

slowly diffusing new colour

a dreamlike path

today a forest dweller was sent ahead

to clear a path for you

fuelled by yesterday's words

you whispered into earth

thursday you forgot this power

so friday you were hemmed in

not remembering that tomorrow will unravel

according to what you spoke

and that reality

lies buried in the softness

of your mouth

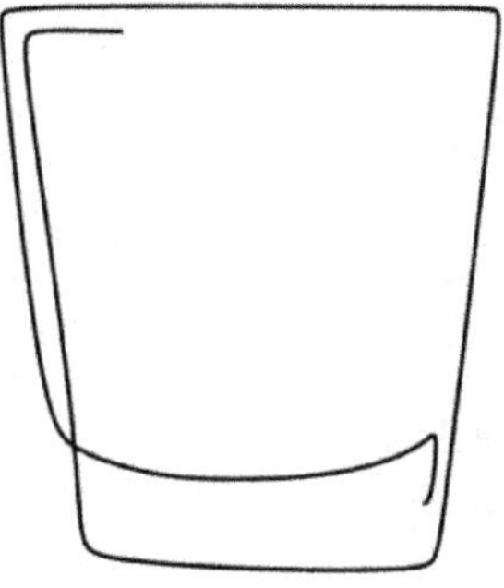

concerning the sweetness of our mothers

when the strange man came knocking

in the blackness of the night

asking for the landlord,

you lit the lamp and prayed until

the room was beaming

with a different light

the glow of safety

enshrouded us

and we were suspended in it

by the time your blessed lips

had finished their plea

my grandmother cooked a blossom

the french constellations bore the brunt of my searching gazes
on that day my grandmother cooked a blossom
floral scent billowed through the apartment
past the folded blankets encased in clear plastic zip bags
past the decorated metal plates from a souk in marrakesh
both of us dissolving, both of us diffusing into air and becoming
annihilated, nothing. both emitting for the first time the scent
of Divine purpose. stirring pink petals in a blackened pot
stirring a blackened heart with a newfound love and light
on that day, my grandmother cooked a blossom

rosary

the rosary outlasted him. my mother forgot his name

but she murmured he was a pious man

i thumb through each black orb, counting the time

breath and matter, life and death, another human story

with the same rosary that made its way to me

that may outlive my fingers

purchase these nights before they purchase you

rain pouring into the lake at lordship rec

and a hundred and one purple clouds pulsating-

the edge of our galaxy almost visible

through the london smog

this is the stuff of life, the *baraka* is in the

small things, small witnessings

but these things are larger, out lasted pharaoh,

qarun, do you hear the laughter

of ozymandias?

origami lungs

it has already happened.
this is why you feel
the golden warmth
of familiarity

an ancient decree
has unfolded
around you
inside you
origami lungs contract
to give it room

so sudden
it has momentarily
electrocuted sense
natural enough
for the wise body
to withstand

clay

don't snag
on the teeth
of the form
reality has taken
clay can only hold
for so long
add muddy water
and spin your self
don't dry out

pass through
quickly
soon you will
come to know
when *qadr*
decrees the day
tired clay cracks,
relinquishes
and life
begins

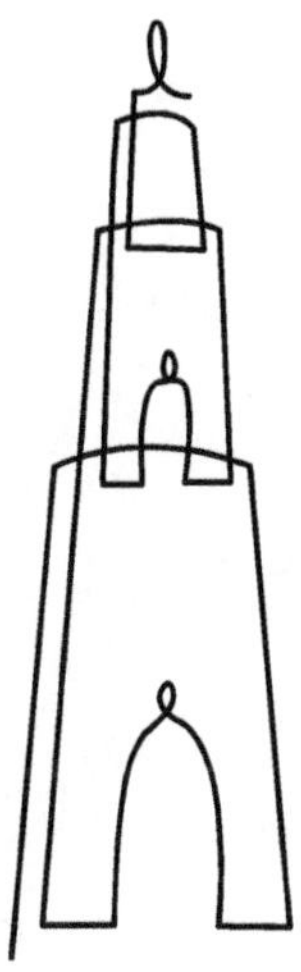

silkworm

silkworm,

we all have to die a little

to spin a little silk,

and we are displaced people,

destitute

eternal home is our words and actions -

when light enters

through the wound

know simultaneously opportunity

escapes it

where suddenly silver dust

becomes manifest

in the atmosphere

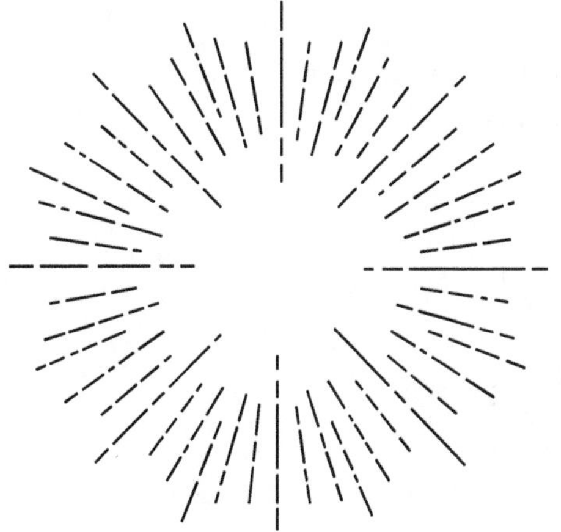

happiness

conscious air softly bellows a frequency

that observes my still prayer

momentarily,

a moment of *haqq*:

nothing and everything holds me upright

tenderly,

and the earth is my prayer mat

naturally,

and creation moves with me and unfolds around me

unequivocally,

and He is certainly the Most High.

42

part two: by africa,
the iridescence of her beauty

by the quiver of an arrow

by the quiver of an arrow

by the richness of repeated promises for tomorrow

by the cassava leaves bowing to an ascending sun

by the cracked heel of the sheikh who does not know he is one

by the song of the saint hiding in the cough of the sick

by the abyss of the amphitheatre after curtains conclude this shift

by africa, the iridescence of her beauty

and the opals at her neck

by the flight of her swallows

and the majesty of her subjects

by the breath of dawn, by a city's silent sleep

by faith, and the renaissance

by never accepting defeat

by the smiling origin.

by the smiling origin, the origin,

the origin.

ruins

for the ruins of mali

for the remnants of amina's walls

for the resistance of the vanguard

who never die, and always multiply

for that struggle that was thrust into the face

of every new-born noble

for growing up a seedling between the world and me

for the falconers who have never heard the falcon

for the centre that has never held

for the family crest that is not cotton, that is

instead iron, for iron teeth

for iron souls, housing iron wills

for skeletons propping muscular bodies, fortified

by iron

for the cadres and the comrades, the flesh

that passed through cape coast

for that that flesh too luminescent too honourable to remain

for our long long antennae, for the

promise of summer,

for keeping my eyes glassy and

warm

for me east facing a blood orange sun

for waiting on that first fist

to rupture

from beneath my feet

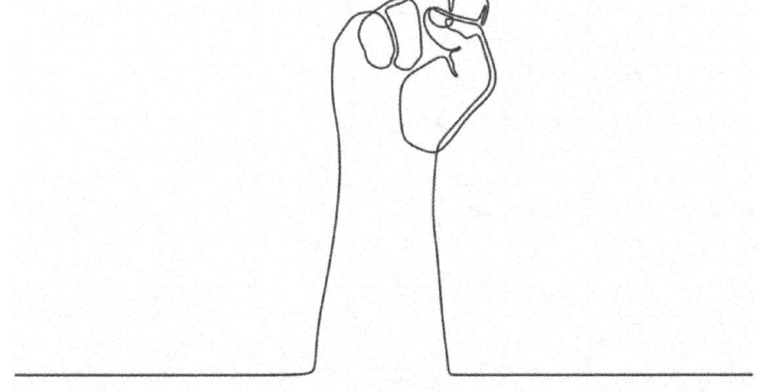

equator

tracing fingers delicately along dotted lines
on an aqua globe in a bookshop basement

in the basement of the heart
cartographies of dispossession occupy the rhythm

a now binaural rhythm of decorated feet stamping outside of the body
mimic the complex strings of the ancient soul being played

playing outside on a north london street
memories of dried powder paint and sugar paper come flooding back

back and forth and to and fro the mother rocks the baby
and to and fro and back and forth tender fingers assemble the cradle

you are the cradle and the origin
you are the beginning of the beginning

me beginning as soil of your soil
clay of your clay

will end as clay of your clay
soil of your soil

accra sunset

i imagine you smell like orange peel

the kind that kojo used to leave on the ground

after a game of oware with the men

those men outside j & r supermarket

that one near total - dansoman

zest mixed with dust mixed with diesel

warm like the body of a fat squirming newborn

bathed in the perfume of the 'oohs' and 'aahs'

of crowding faces-

her first sleep in this life

during the throbbing humidity

of kwahu rainfall

a symphony of car horns

rising to a crescendo

when stacked suitcases, baskets and lampposts

make a slow pilgrimage

to frame your ascent

the winters of past days could never

have prepared me for this.

not this.

not all this gorgeous life

part two: by africa, the iridescence of her beauty

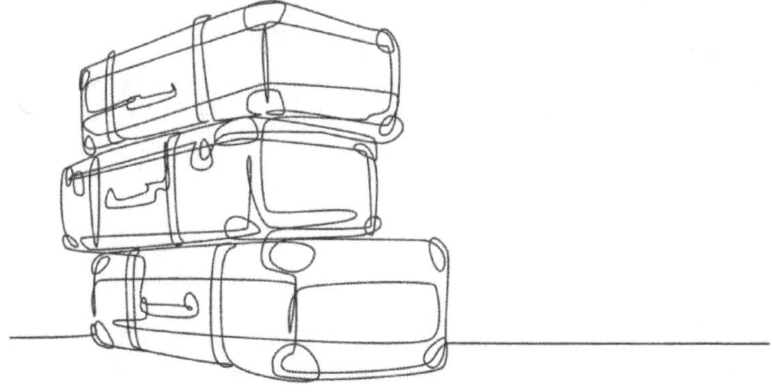

the carpet weaver

woven brown rug
resting stark on victorian floorboards
assembled with the mechanical precision
of the unskilled subaltern

a jaded tapestry of sorts;
brown hues; beige highlights;
black undertones

ridged at the touch
like the glistening foreheads
of the nuer, or the
calluses of our parents-
ifaniyi's ring binder
always the trailing scent
of bamboo

bump after bump, hurdle
after trough
knot after loophole:
the bureaucracy
facing the carpet weaver
and the asylum seeker
a labour of love, one
we allow careless feet
to greet

boats and bilqees

bilqees taught me to read qur'an

i would sound out tentative

before speaking foreign matter

into air

when i closed my eyes

i would see, *Alif Lām Mīm*

and dwell on rules i couldn't understand

i share this with you all

because a green boat

has since come to collect me

i saw a ghanaian fisherman

moored on the thames

and i didn't think twice

as i sailed away

the textbooks of the scholars

it whimpers an elegy for itself, gnashing and clawing

its comrades above ground try to revive it, but the beast is ailing

"the sun has set on ghana", the slippery tongue slithers

and speaks in ink to record this astonishing utterance

causing both the flight of an eagle and a steely sky to freeze

in appalled silence

kofi believes it for fifty years, through his own visitation

is released from the lashing claws of that sickly beast,

not enough to rescue a stolen lifetime locked, labelled

and archived in a library of deceit

pan to a frothing atlantic, where that slouching thing

is chained to the seabed. the textbooks of the scholars

cabral and sankara, a preserved light in the belly of timbuktu

black rebellion in darkness upon bottomless darkness has blinded it

in a clearing, stoic elders bare toothless smiles

and the eagles and the african djinn kind assemble to listen:

"we believe the vanguard will win one day

one day the vanguard will win"

if forty-four sunsets have made us sad, then the forty fourth sunrise

laughing from the east, is surely and axiom for glory

the alien

there is nothing fanciful nor arbitrary

about the man who speaks six languages, but belongs

to nowhere

abandoned at every border and taking

unsheltered earth as home

a fragile being knocking on city doors only

to be boxed up and safely thrown

onto rotating doorsteps

undulating cadence with no airs or graces

a professor of the streets or a student of

desertion

slinking between raindrops and draining into gutters

orphaned by misjudged opportunity

and dreams of diasporic glory

now one bleary eye searching for police

and the other

for all twelve of him.

nothing fanciful, nothing fanciful at all

nothing fanciful about the land of the lost

or the liturgy of the lonely

the postal address being beneath bridges

and between buildings or behind bushes under

breaking skies

how powerful is the man who has died every

night, and knows
the colour of gratitude

even during the rupture of waking
from the home of his weary slumber

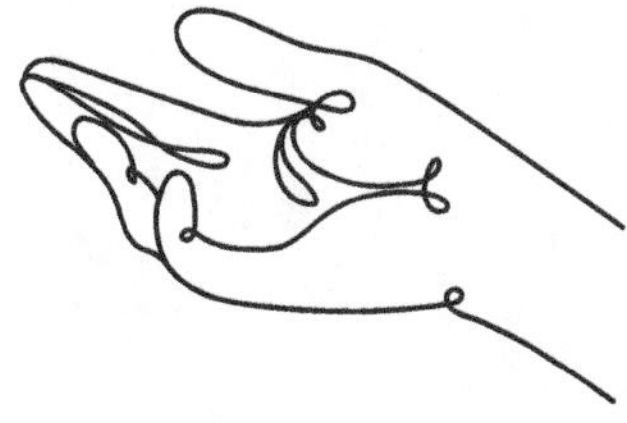

wagadou

calling the tremor of a kingdom

preserved in the lilt of omar jabbie

traversing the market babble

and trade of the departed

now reaching plastic headphones

on a london bus

wagadou, home clay

born liberated

shackled in created space

and lines that confine

floors that support feet and

ceilings that cave in around us

muscular nobles caught-

contained according to custom

contained by ink and paper

the victor unwrites us

and bleeds black onto parchment

folded paper contorts

the illustration of our hero

until he too becomes a crumpled shadow

a nation, printed into deserted textbooks

and folded into a box

systemic creases now denting the surface

of a once smooth page

not the nourishing kind that

fills with water to feed livestock

but the kind that fills with dirt and debris

more and more opaque

muddy clay is born liberated,

from adama to adam

all four earths combine to birth

all of humankind

yet how to deliver

captured mind from lines

how to rescue clouded eyes

from a corrugated void-

mahogany

wooden skin, tougher than the soles of

cobalt children, traceable age in circular rings

forming at the knuckle, and elbow

least noticeable at the knee-

unvarnished. skincare is not

a pastime of the proletariat:

nor is self-care

nonetheless the skin has a rustic flair-

no?

double the auction price

sell to corporate brokers

because a canvas of discolouring

hangs in the office of an art dealer

and the man that built his corner desk

is carved from madagascan mahogany

ohema, daughter of the sun

hibiscus

a sandstorm swirls behind each iris

and on each cheek

an orange moon

waxing and waning

a pitch-dark galaxy has tumbled into your lap,

and has sunken into your skin

tomorrow's promise-

ohema,

daughter of the sun.

Illustration acknowledgments

Olga Ubirailo, page 9
Sadesign9, page 9
Sketchify, pages 15, 17, 19, 21, 23, 29, 32, 33, 35,37, 39, 53, 65
Aisha Nuraini, pages 24, 31, 41, 49, 51, 61
Rizqisani, page 27
Oleksandra Kalenychenko, page 30
Iuliia Belova, page 45
Ahmad Safarudin, page 47
Projectmarketingkv, page 55
Anker, page 57
gstudioimagen2, page 59
Paulina Shakirova, page 63
Irina Shisterova page 64

www.ingramcontent.com/pod-product-compliance
Lightning Source LLC
Chambersburg PA
CBHW050815050726
47601CB00019B/281/J